FUN FINDING OUT

ME AND MY BODY

Rosie McCormick   Anthony Lewis

KINGFISHER

To Johanna – RMC
To Stephen – AL

KINGFISHER
Kingfisher Publications Plc
New Penderel House, 283-288 High Holborn, London WC1V 7HZ

First published in paperback by Kingfisher Publications Plc 1998
10 9 8 7 6 5 4 3 2 1

ISBN 0 7534 0297 1

The rights of Rosie McCormick to be identified as author
of this book and Anthony Lewis to be identified as illustrator
of this book have been asserted by them in accordance with
the Copyright, Designs and Patents Act, 1988.

Series editor: Sue Nicholson
Series designer: Kathryn Caulfield
Printed in Singapore

Answers

Staying healthy
1 Drink water; 2 Eat healthy food; 3 Exercise;
4 Get plenty of sleep

Seeing is believing
1 The two lines are the same length – the arrows
on the ends of each line make us think the one
on the left is longer.
2 You may be able to see white arrows AND black
arrows!

Things that help the doctor
Stethoscope – to listen to your breathing or
hear your heart beating; Torch – so the doctor can
see into your ears or down your throat;
Thermometer – to take your temperature

Contents

Fingers

Hand

Arm

Head

Neck

Waist

Hips

Leg

Knee

Ankle

Foot

Toes

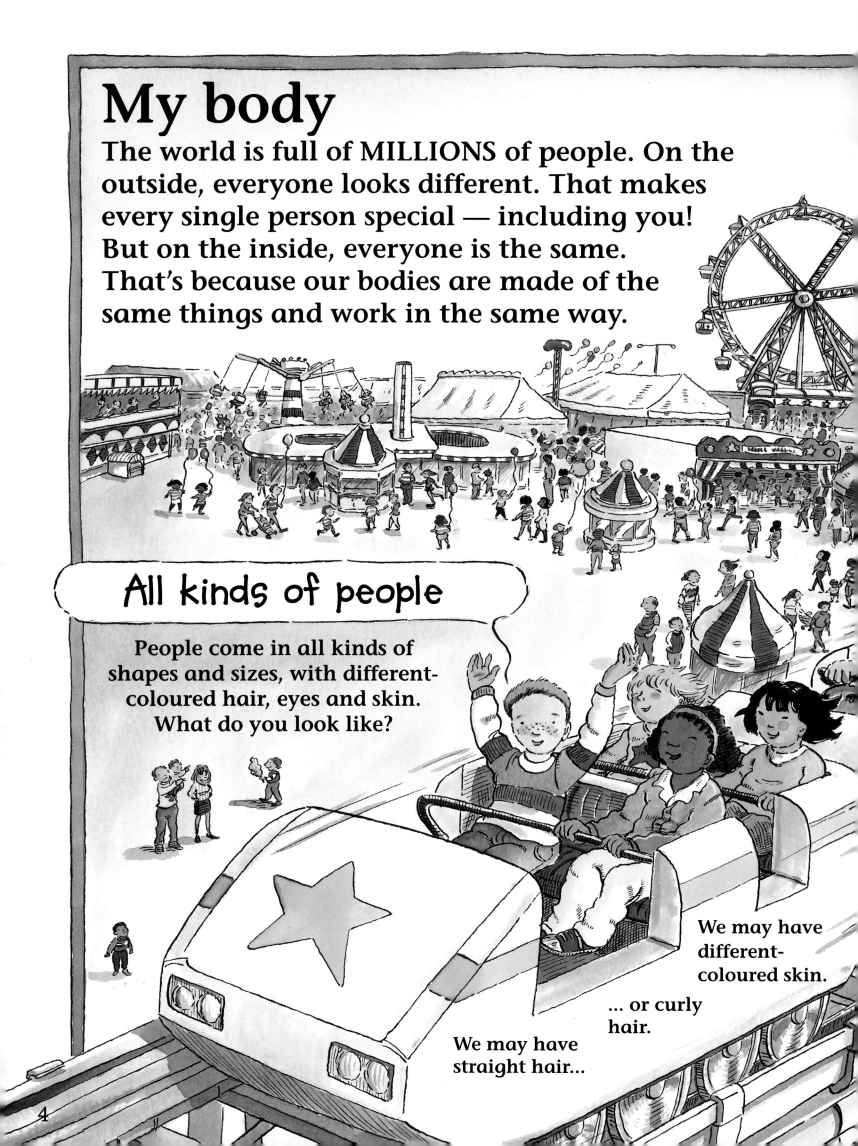

My body

The world is full of MILLIONS of people. On the outside, everyone looks different. That makes every single person special — including you! But on the inside, everyone is the same. That's because our bodies are made of the same things and work in the same way.

All kinds of people

People come in all kinds of shapes and sizes, with different-coloured hair, eyes and skin. What do you look like?

We may have different-coloured skin.

... or curly hair.

We may have straight hair...

4

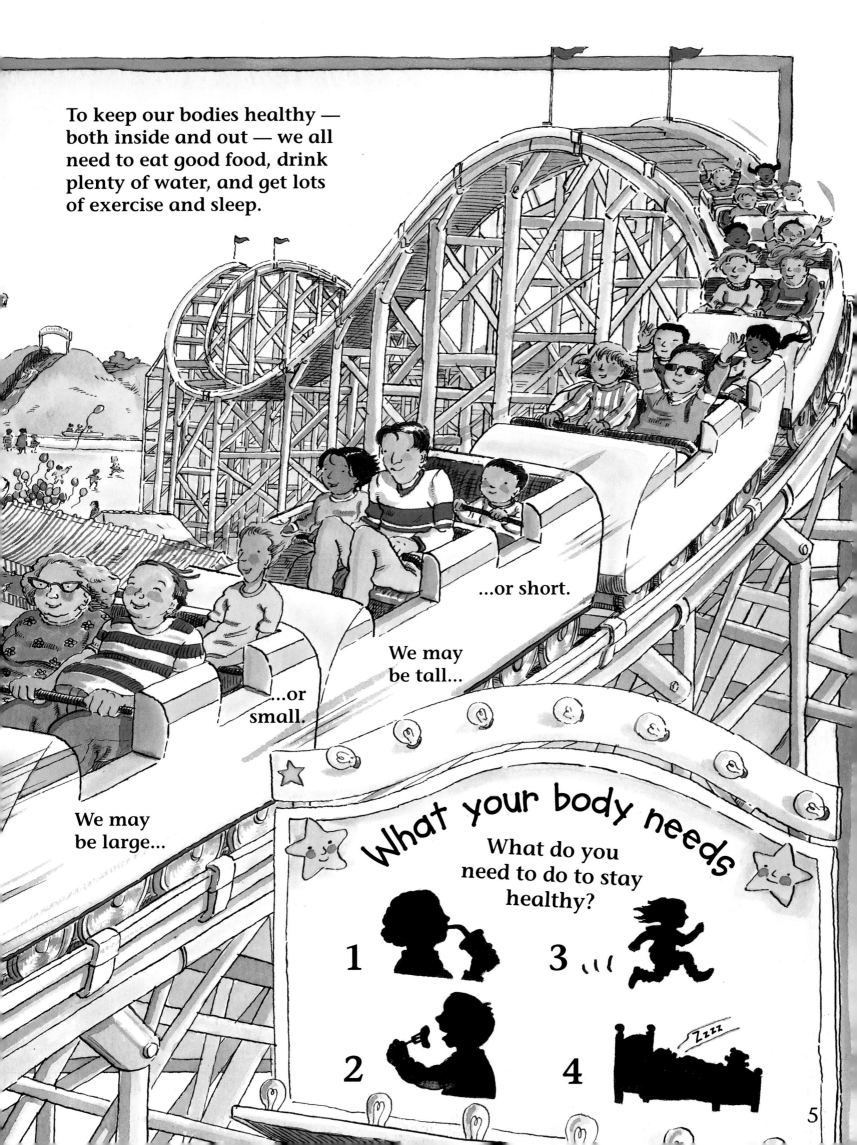

To keep our bodies healthy —
both inside and out — we all
need to eat good food, drink
plenty of water, and get lots
of exercise and sleep.

...or short.

We may
be tall...

...or
small.

We may
be large...

What your body needs

**What do you
need to do to stay
healthy?**

1

2

3

4

5

My muscles and bones

The bones in your body give you shape and hold you up. Without them, you would fall over like a wobbly jelly! Bones also protect the softer parts inside your body, such as your brain. Your muscles move your bones about so you can walk, wave, run and jump.

Your muscles are attached to your bones by strong stringy bands called tendons.

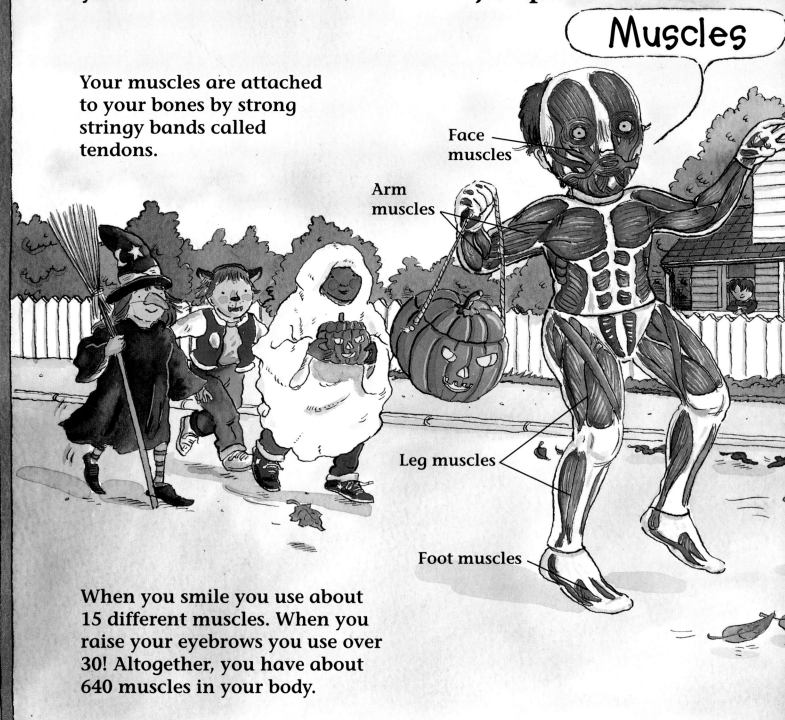

Muscles

Face muscles

Arm muscles

Leg muscles

Foot muscles

When you smile you use about 15 different muscles. When you raise your eyebrows you use over 30! Altogether, you have about 640 muscles in your body.

Bones

Your bones join together in places called joints, so you can bend and move.

Skull

Hand bones

Arm bones

Elbow joint

Ribs

Breastbone

Backbone

Hip bones

Thighbone

Knee joint

Ankle joint

Foot bones

When you are born, you have about 350 bones in your body. As you grow, some of the small bones join together to make bigger ones. You end up with just over 200 bones.

My heart and lungs

Dub–dub, dub–dub, dub–dub...

If you touch your chest firmly, you can feel your heart beating. As it beats, your heart is pumping blood all around your body. Your lungs supply your blood with oxygen from the air you breathe.

Sneezing helps to keep your nose clear so you can breathe properly. You yawn when your body needs to take in more oxygen.

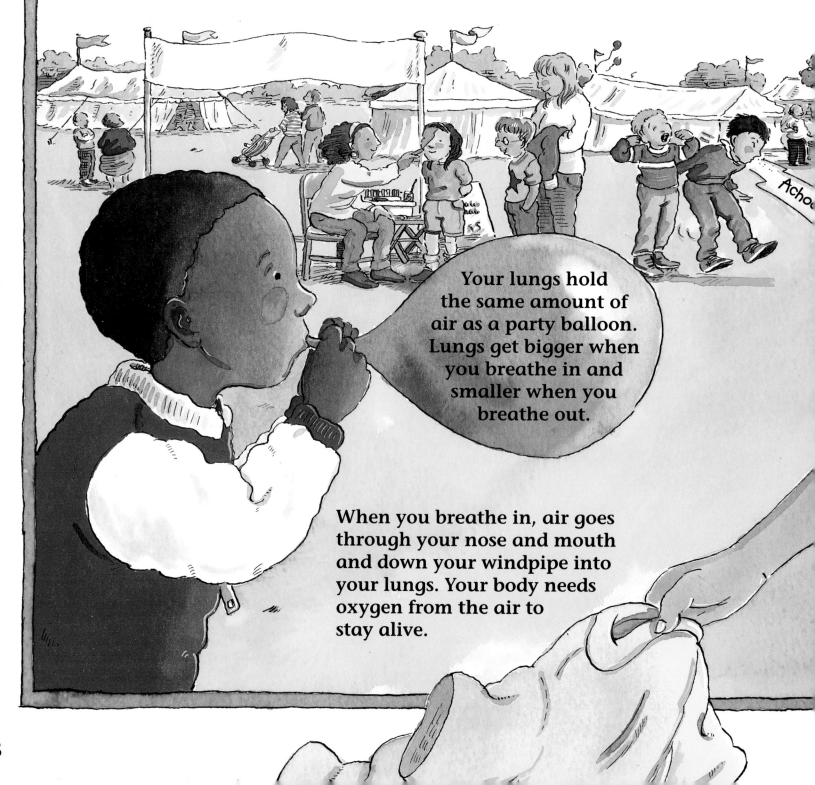

Your lungs hold the same amount of air as a party balloon. Lungs get bigger when you breathe in and smaller when you breathe out.

When you breathe in, air goes through your nose and mouth and down your windpipe into your lungs. Your body needs oxygen from the air to stay alive.

8

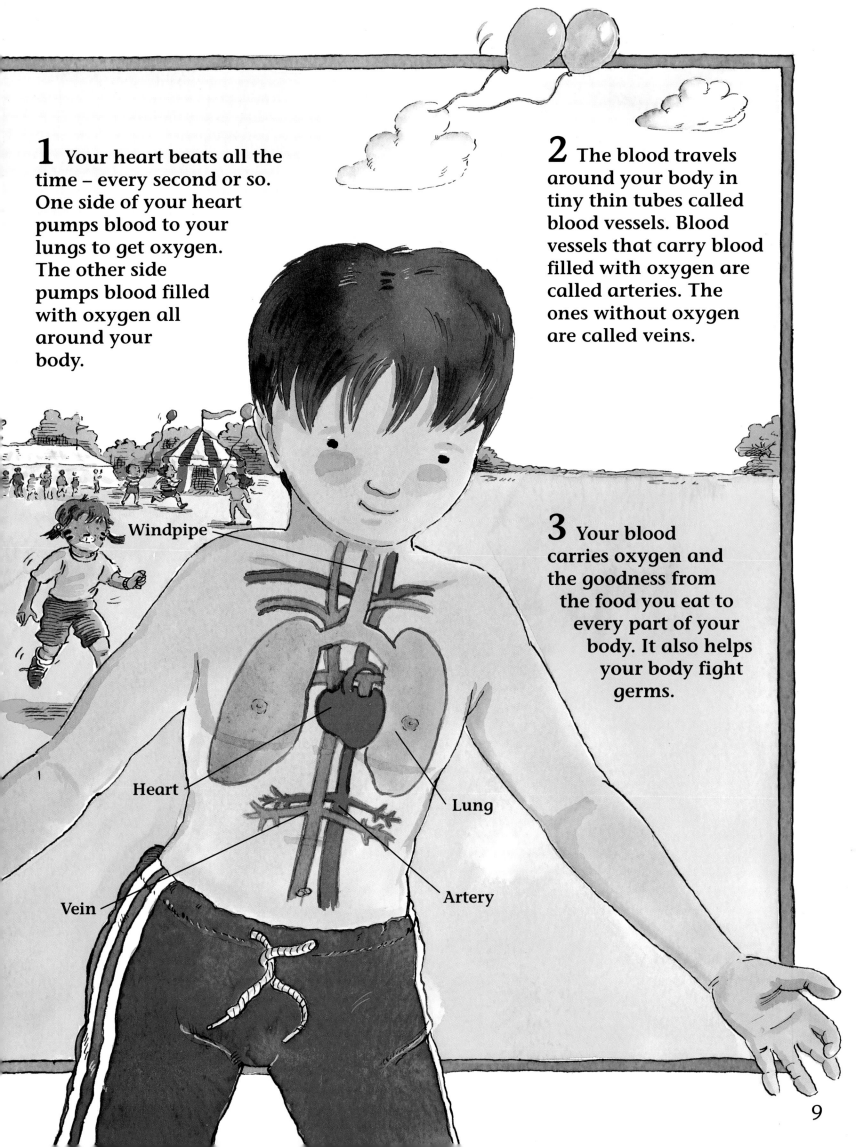

1 Your heart beats all the time – every second or so. One side of your heart pumps blood to your lungs to get oxygen. The other side pumps blood filled with oxygen all around your body.

2 The blood travels around your body in tiny thin tubes called blood vessels. Blood vessels that carry blood filled with oxygen are called arteries. The ones without oxygen are called veins.

3 Your blood carries oxygen and the goodness from the food you eat to every part of your body. It also helps your body fight germs.

Windpipe

Heart

Vein

Lung

Artery

9

My brain

Inside your head, protected by your skull, is your brain. Your brain is very important because it controls everything you do. It takes in information and sends out signals to the rest of your body, telling it how to work.

Your brain is about half the size of your head. It looks just like a crinkly walnut.

Brain power

Your brain helps you to remember things. Look at these pictures then cover them up. How many can you remember?

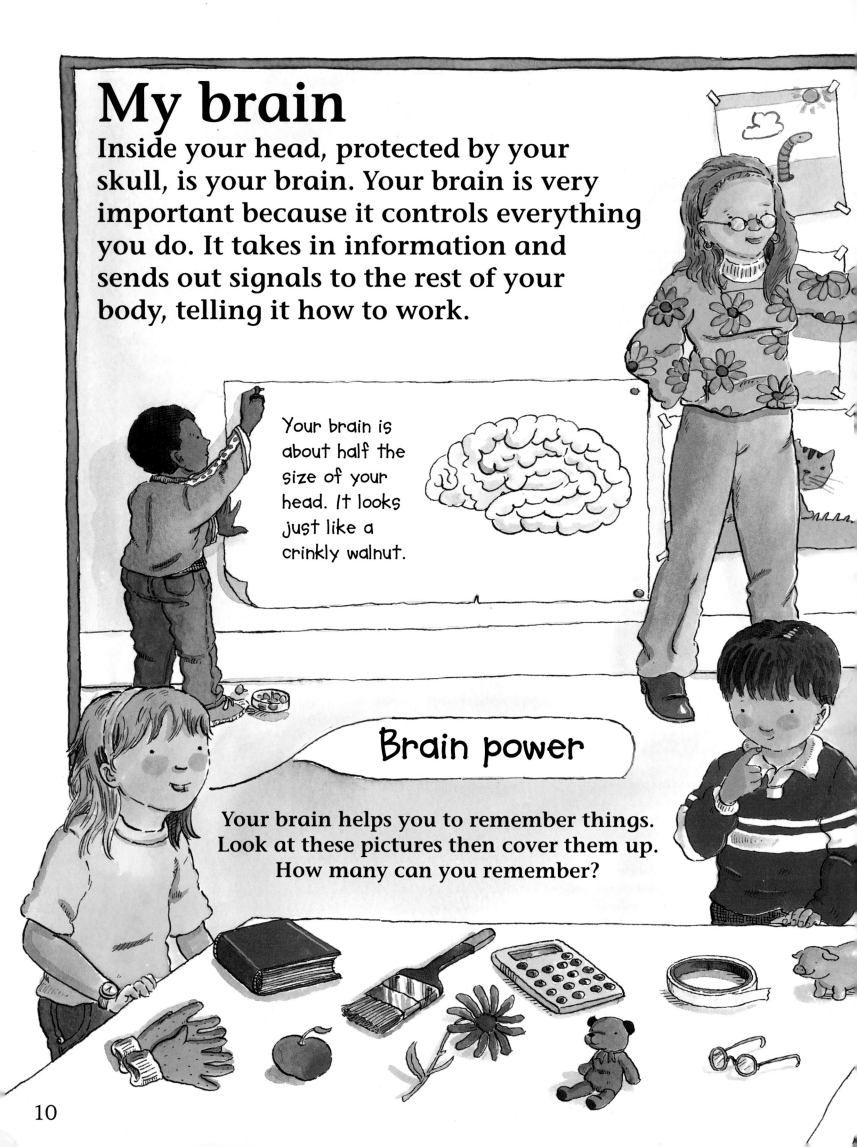

Parts of the brain

Your brain is divided up into different parts.
Each part has a different job to do.

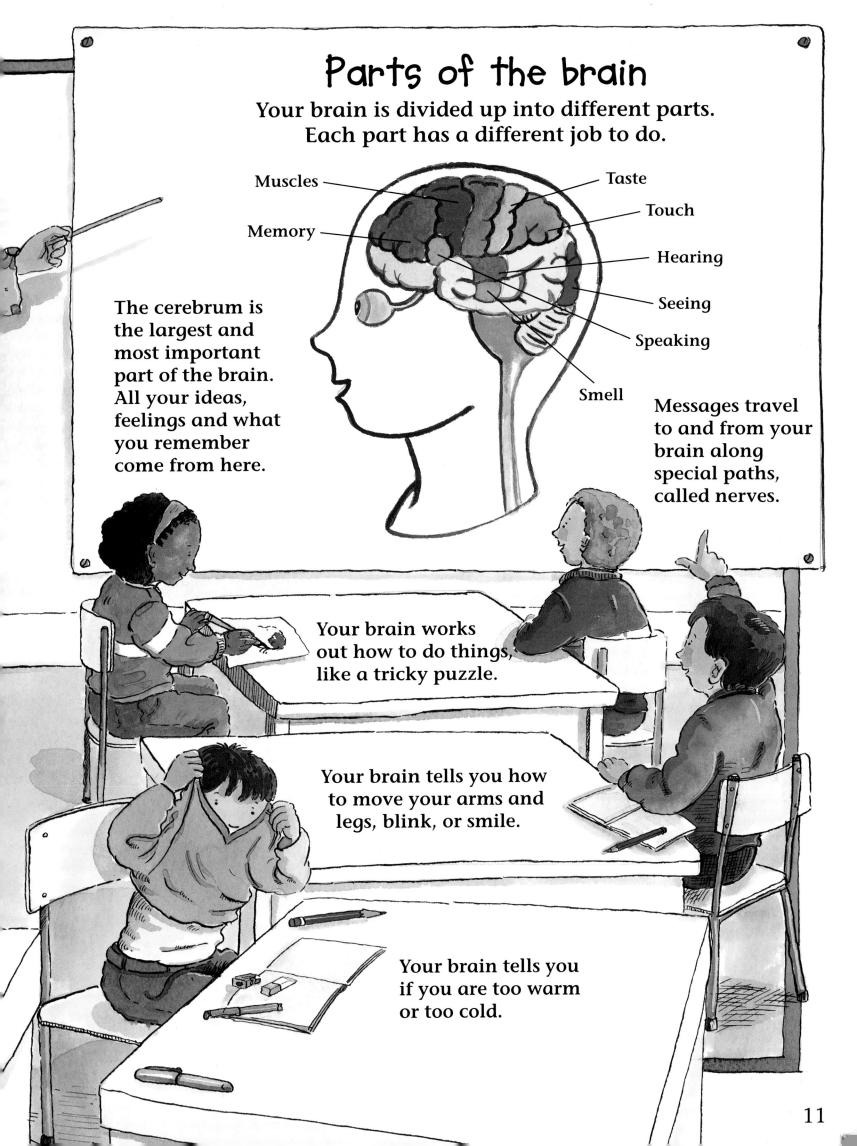

Muscles

Taste

Touch

Memory

Hearing

Seeing

Speaking

Smell

The cerebrum is the largest and most important part of the brain. All your ideas, feelings and what you remember come from here.

Messages travel to and from your brain along special paths, called nerves.

Your brain works out how to do things, like a tricky puzzle.

Your brain tells you how to move your arms and legs, blink, or smile.

Your brain tells you if you are too warm or too cold.

11

My skin

Your skin is quite amazing. It covers your body, from the top of your head to the tip of your toes, and it grows with you as you grow. It protects you from germs and injuries. And it keeps your insides where they ought to be — inside your body.

Skin is very sensitive to the sun's rays and may get burned. Sun creams help to protect it.

Everyone's skin contains a substance called melanin. Melanin is a natural protection from the sun. Dark skin has more melanin than light skin.

The hair on your head also helps to protect you from the sun.

Your skin is waterproof. It stops water getting into your body.

Healing skin

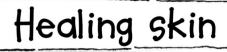

If you cut yourself, your skin can heal itself.

1 Your blood forms a scab to cover the damaged area.

2 New skin starts to grow underneath the scab.

3 When the wound has healed, the scab falls off.

The skin on your fingers and toes is covered in a pattern of tiny swirly lines. These are your fingerprints and toeprints. No one else has the same prints as you.

Underneath your skin are millions of tiny nerves that send out messages.

Nerves tell your brain whether you are touching something rough or smooth, hot or cold — or whether it hurts!

My ears

Crash, bang, wallop!

Your ears can hear all kinds of sounds, from a loud yell to a quiet whisper. Listening to sounds helps us to understand what is happening in the world around us.

As well as being able to hear, most people can see, smell, taste and touch. These are our senses. They allow us to listen to music, read a book, enjoy a tasty meal or feel a fluffy kitten's fur!

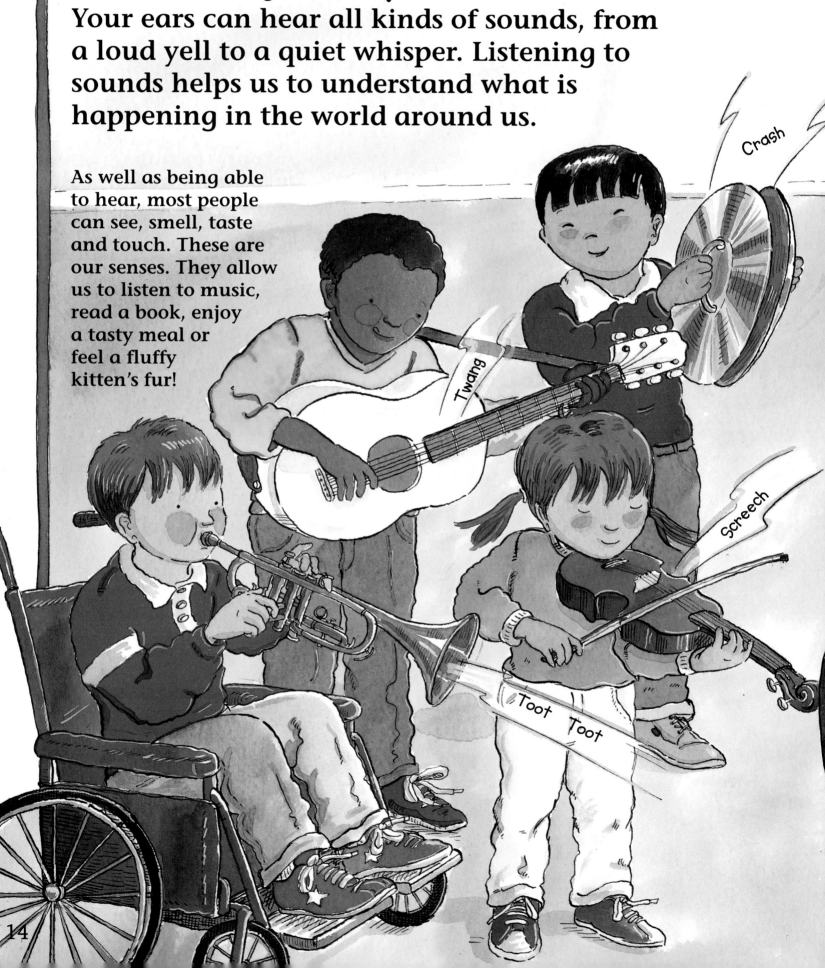

Crash

Twang

Screech

Toot Toot

Your ears don't just hear sounds, they also help you to balance. Inside your ears are special tubes filled with liquid. When you jump about, the liquid swirls around, too. As it moves, it sends messages to your brain, letting it know if you need extra help to stay on your feet!

How we hear

Our ears are funnel-shaped to catch sounds from the air.

Hammer bone

Nerves carry messages to the brain

Anvil bone

Stirrup bone

Eardrum

Ear

1 Sounds enter your ear and make your eardrum, and the three tiny bones behind it, move to and fro.

2 A liquid deep in your ear then moves, too. Nerves feel this movement and send signals to your brain.

15

My eyes

When it's dark, it's difficult to see. When it's sunny and bright, or when you turn on the light, you can see quite clearly. That's because your eyes need light to help them to see.

How we see

Eyeball

Retina

The lens helps your eyes to focus.

Your whole eye is shaped like a ball.

When you look at something, an upside down picture of it appears on the back of your eyeball. Nerves send a message about the picture to your brain, and your brain turns it the right way up.

Seeing is believing

Sometimes our eyes play tricks on us. Look at these pictures.

Which line is longer?   Are the arrows black or white?

Light and dark

In bright light, your pupils become smaller so they don't take in too much light and dazzle you.

In dim light, your pupils become larger so that they can take in more light and you can see better.

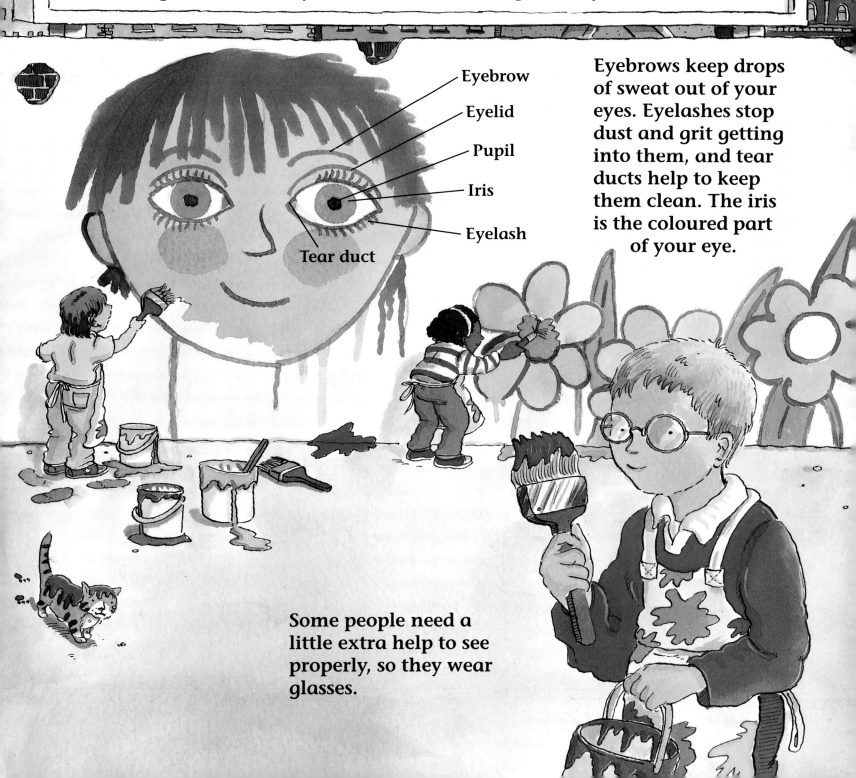

Eyebrow

Eyelid

Pupil

Iris

Eyelash

Tear duct

Eyebrows keep drops of sweat out of your eyes. Eyelashes stop dust and grit getting into them, and tear ducts help to keep them clean. The iris is the coloured part of your eye.

Some people need a little extra help to see properly, so they wear glasses.

My nose and tongue

Your nose helps you to smell things, such as a smelly drain, or a sweetly scented flower. Your tongue helps you to taste things, such as a delicious chocolate ice cream. It also helps you to speak and sing.

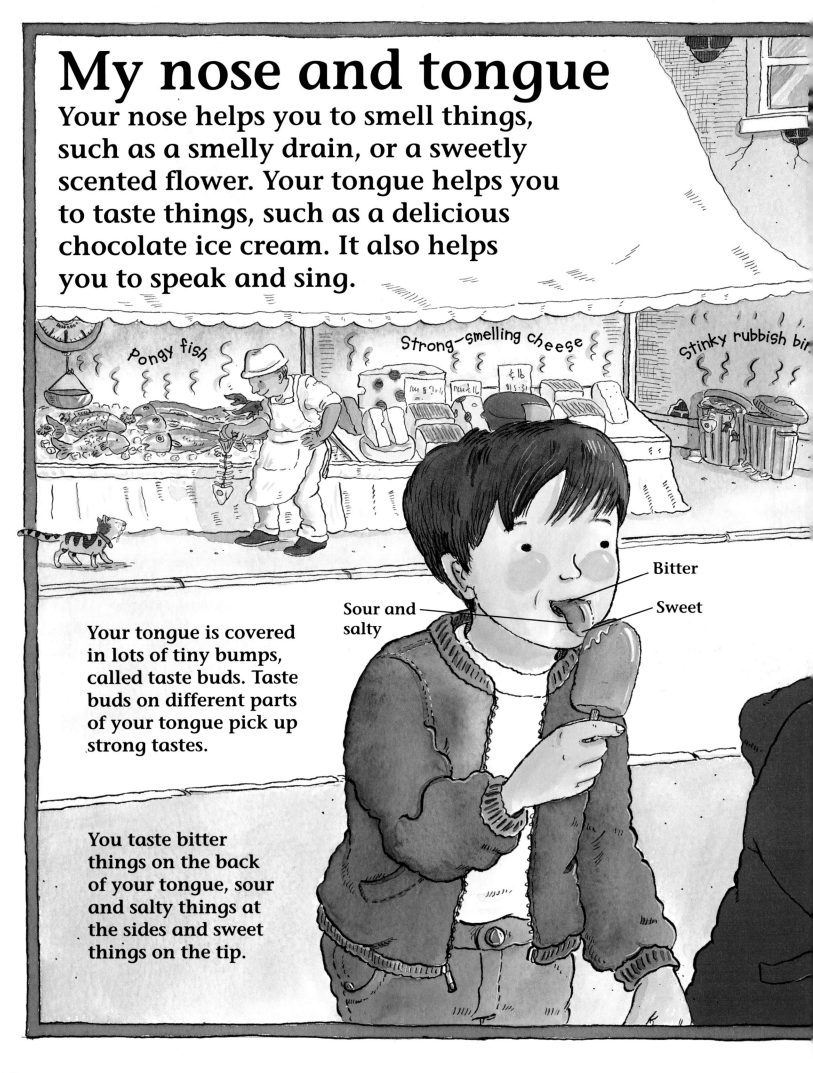

Pongy fish

Strong-smelling cheese

Stinky rubbish bin

Bitter

Sour and salty

Sweet

Your tongue is covered in lots of tiny bumps, called taste buds. Taste buds on different parts of your tongue pick up strong tastes.

You taste bitter things on the back of your tongue, sour and salty things at the sides and sweet things on the tip.

Smoky fumes

Sweet-smelling flowers

Find out how important your tongue is for speaking. Hold the tip of your tongue between your thumb and first finger and try to say "hello". Can you speak clearly?

When you have a cold your nose sometimes gets bunged up. This stops you smelling — and enjoying — your food.

Smelly drains

Your sense of smell is *much* stronger than your sense of taste. Without it, you cannot taste your food properly. Try holding your nose when you eat a tasty snack. Can you taste it?

My tummy

Munch, munch, crunch!

After you have smelled, tasted and chewed your food, you swallow it. The food then travels through long winding pipes and tubes — all the way from your mouth to your bottom.

1 First, the food travels down a food pipe called a gullet. When it reaches your tummy it is squashed and mashed into a pulpy soup.

2 The pulp is then squeezed through a long winding tube called your intestine. As it moves along the intestine, tiny bits of food are taken into your blood and carried around your body to give it energy.

3 The parts of the food that your body does not want, or cannot use, are pushed along to the colon at the end of your intestine.

Gullet

Liver

Tummy

Intestine

Colon

When you burp, air rushes back up your gullet from your tummy. Fizzy, bubbly drinks often make people burp.

When you go to the bathroom, the waste food stored in your intestine passes out of your body through your bottom.

Burp

A meal can take up to three whole days to pass all the way through your body.

Kidneys

Rumble

Your kidneys help to get rid of waste water, called urine, and your liver helps to break down food.

When your tummy has been empty for a while, it may fill with gas and rumble. A rumbling tummy often means you're hungry!

21

My teeth

Going to the dentist is very important. The dentist helps to keep your teeth and gums healthy. You need healthy teeth and gums to slice and chew your food so that you can swallow it.

Your teeth are made of a very hard bone-like material.

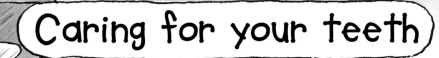

It is important to brush your teeth every morning and evening, as well as after meals.

If you do not brush away the tiny bits of food that collect on and around your teeth, your teeth may rot or decay.

22

The story of teeth
Our teeth change as we get older.

1 When you are born you have no teeth at all, just hard gums.

2 By the time you are two, you have about 20 teeth, called "milk" teeth.

3 When you are about six, your milk teeth fall out. Larger, adult teeth grow underneath.

Kinds of teeth

Sharp incisors are for cutting food.

Pointed canines are for tearing.

Big molars are used for grinding and crushing.

Sometimes, as your adult teeth grow, they become crooked. The dentist may put a brace on them to straighten them.

23

When I am ill

There are times when you feel ill. Perhaps your tummy hurts, or you have a cough, or even spots. Sometimes you are ill because germs have got inside your body. So, a visit to the doctor, and some medicine, will help.

Fighting germs

Germs are tiny living things that float in the air and in water. They are sometimes found in food too!

Most germs can't hurt you, but some can make you ill. Your body fights and kills off germs.

Things that help the doctor
What does a doctor use these for?

Stethoscope   Torch   Thermometer

24

1 The doctor may take your temperature with a thermometer to find out how hot you are.

2 The doctor might listen to your heart and chest through a stethoscope.

3 Sometimes the doctor looks into your ears and throat with a special torch.

Some diseases, such as chickenpox and mumps, are very easy to catch, but you usually only catch them once. After that, your body learns how to protect itself against them.

Sometimes you are given an injection so you don't get ill. No one likes having an injection because it pricks, but it doesn't hurt for long.

Staying healthy

Your body needs your help to keep it fit and healthy. Eating nutritious food, drinking lots of water, exercising and getting plenty of sleep will all help you to grow big and strong.

Exercise makes your bones, joints and muscles strong. It is also good for your heart and lungs.

Food gives you energy. There are different groups of food and you should eat food from each group every day.

Your body needs lots of water to help it to stay clean on the inside, and keep it working properly.

Keeping clean

It's important to keep your body clean because washing helps to get rid of germs.

Clean your hands and nails before you eat.

Have a bath or shower every day.

Wash your hair to keep it shiny and healthy.

Proteins build strong muscles and bones. We get protein from meat, fish, cheese and milk.

Fibre helps you to digest your food. Fibre comes from fruit, vegetables, cereal and rice.

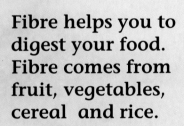

Fats store energy for your body to use. Fats come from milk, cheese and meat.

Carbohydrates give your body energy. They come from bread, cereal, rice and pasta.

Where I come from

Every person in the world begins their life as a tiny baby. Before you were born, you grew inside your mother's tummy in a warm, watery place called the womb. After nine months you were ready to be born.

Sometimes, mums have more than one baby growing inside them. Two babies are called twins.

Goo-ga-goo (How a baby grows)

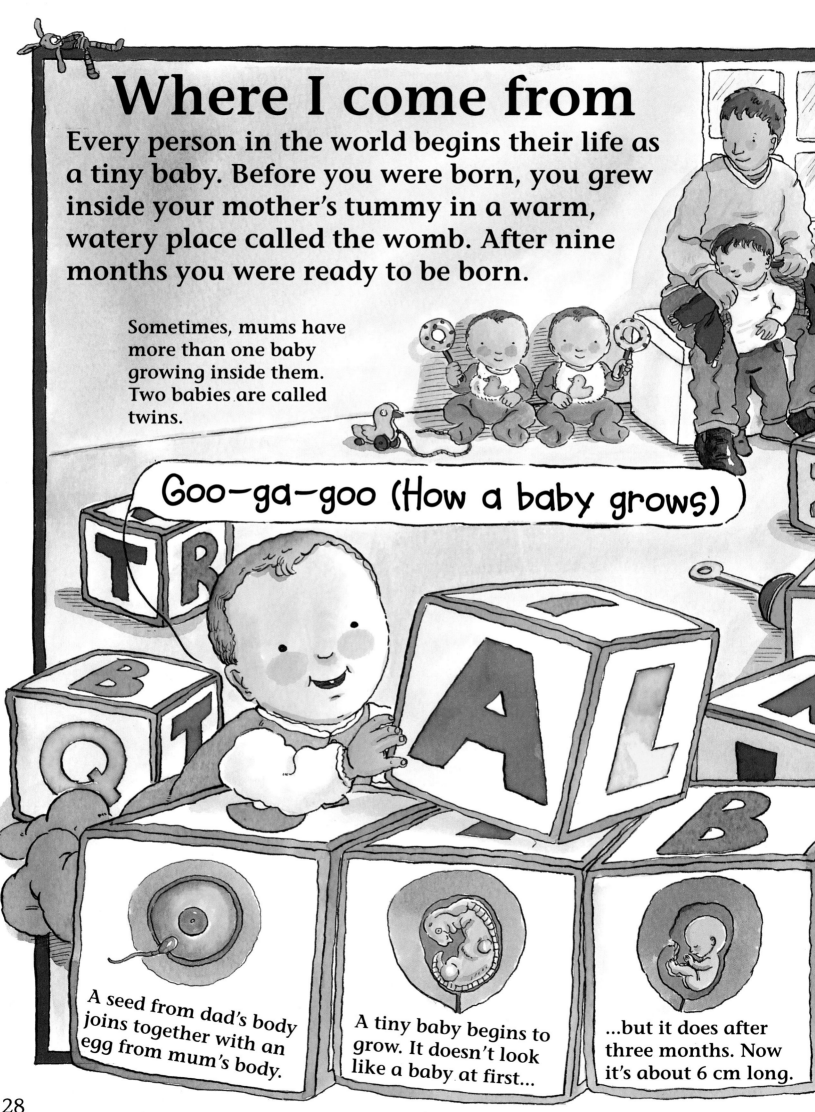

A seed from dad's body joins together with an egg from mum's body.

A tiny baby begins to grow. It doesn't look like a baby at first...

...but it does after three months. Now it's about 6 cm long.

Inside the womb, babies get all the food and oxygen they need through a cord called the umbilical cord. Your tummy button shows you where YOUR cord was once joined to your tummy.

A mother's tummy grows bigger as the baby grows. It protects the baby, keeping it safe and warm.

At five months it starts to move around and begins to kick.

At six months it can suck its thumb and may get hiccups.

At nine months the baby turns upside down.

Growing up

From the moment you are born, until you become a teenager, your body slowly grows and changes.

When you were a brand-new baby, you couldn't do much and needed lots of looking after.

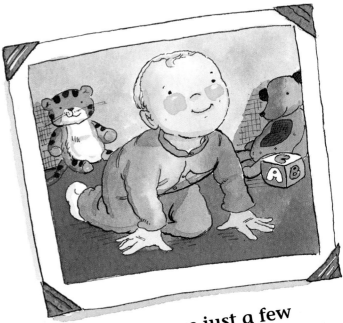

When you were just a few months old, you probably began to sit up and crawl about.

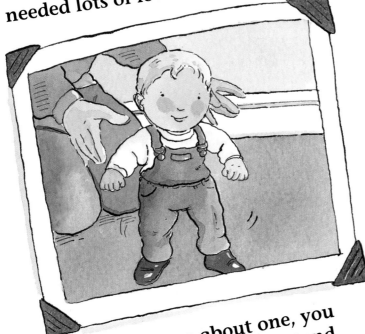

When you were about one, you probably learned how to stand up and began to toddle.

By the time you were three, you could probably run, skip, hop and jump.

Most children go to school when they are five years old. Going to school is a very exciting and important part of growing up.

Just before you become a teenager, when you are about twelve years old, you will notice that your body begins to change.

By the time you become a teenager, you will be taller and heavier. At around eighteen, your body will stop growing, but there will always be new and exciting things to do and learn.

Index